A Step-by-Step Guide
Girls and Boys doi

HOW TO DRAW
PEOPLE
FOR KIDS

Martha Blonde

CONTENTS

Other How to Draw Books
by Martha Blonde

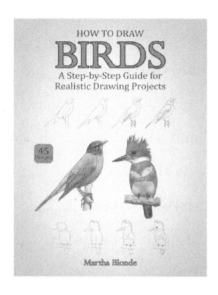

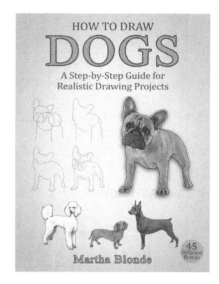

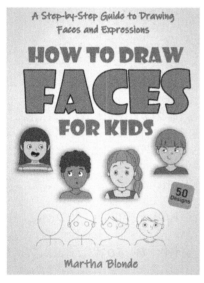

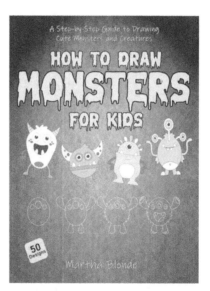

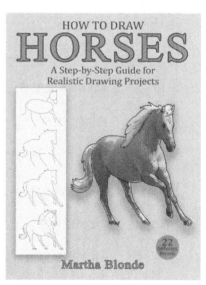

Your support is important!

Dear customer,

We hope you enjoy drawing people with this book. We would be very grateful if you leave us a positive review on Amazon.com. Thank you!

Sincerely,

Martha Blonde

Introduction

"How to Draw People for Kids" is a comprehensive guide for young artists who want to learn how to draw boys and girls in different situations and poses, from playing sports to eating ice cream. Martha Blonde's step-by-step instructions and helpful tips ensure that young artists of all levels will be able to create beautiful illustrations. Whether you're a beginner or a more experienced artist, "How to Draw People for Kids" is the perfect resource to help you develop your creativity and artistic abilities.

This book contains 35 drawing projects of several girls and boys doing different things. In each project you will find two practice spaces with a drawing grid that will help you with your learning path and facilitate your illustration.

Practice with help

Your turn!

Recommended Supplies

Here are some basic tools and materials you will need before starting:

- HB pencils (middle-ground pencils, not too hard not too soft)

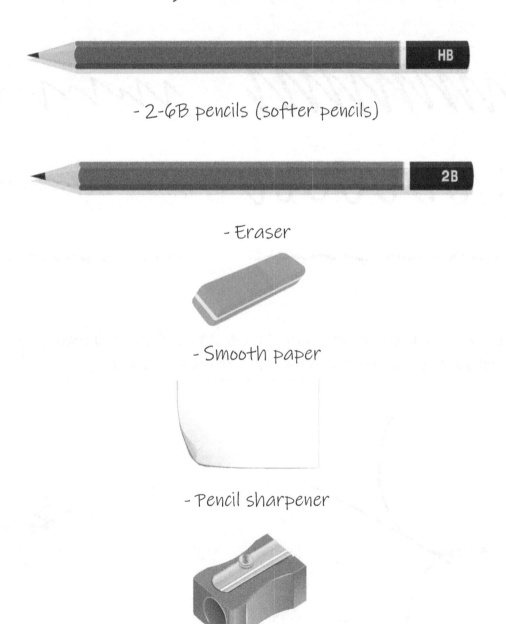

- 2-6B pencils (softer pencils)

- Eraser

- Smooth paper

- Pencil sharpener

Instructions

Before you begin to draw, do some free-flow drawing as warm-up. Remember, people are not perfect, so your drawing does not need to be the same as the step-by-step guide.

Each drawing project has four steps and a facing drawing grid. This grid will help you with the dimension of your drawing.

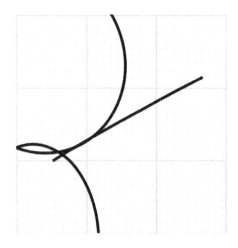 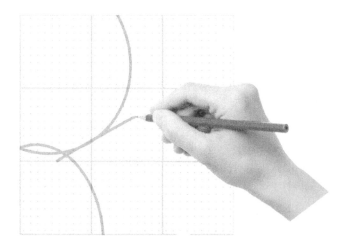

Step by Step

Here you have a quick explanation of each step.

Step 1:
Draw basic shapes (guidelines). This is only to get the drawing's dimension. Afterwards you will erase these lines, so use an HB pencil.

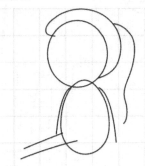

Step 2:
Start drawing the final lines. Start from the top of the head and then move to the body. You should use 2B or 4B pencils.

Step 3:
Complete the drawing. Continue using 2B or 4B pencils. Now you can erase the guidelines from step 1.

Step 4:
Add the details of the hair, clothes, and accessories. You can also add shades if you want a more realistic look.

Remember to sharpen your pencil for better work. When you are done, practice on a new paper, this time without the drawing grid.

Let's draw People!

She is greeting.

Step 1

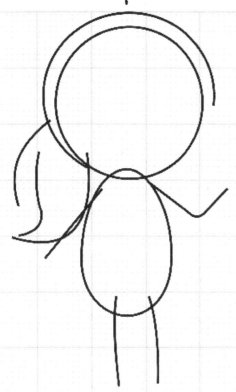

Step 2

Practice with help

Hello!

Step 3

Step 4

Your turn!

He is celebrating.

Step 1

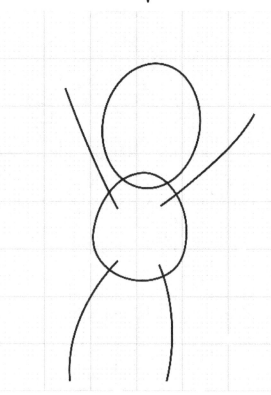

Step 2

Practice
with help

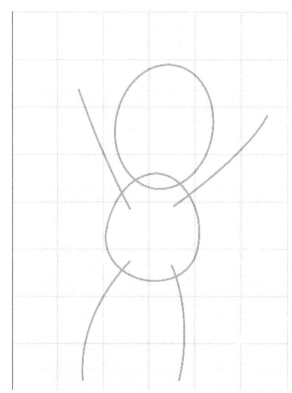

Yeah!

Step 3

Step 4

Your turn!

She is pointing.

Step 1

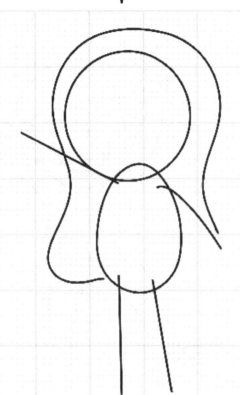

Step 2

Practice
with help

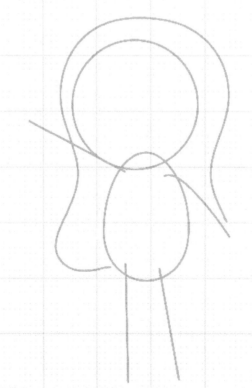

WOW!!!

Step 3

Step 4

Your turn!

He is working out.

Step 1

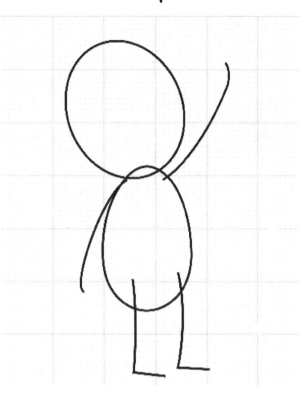

Step 2

Practice
with help

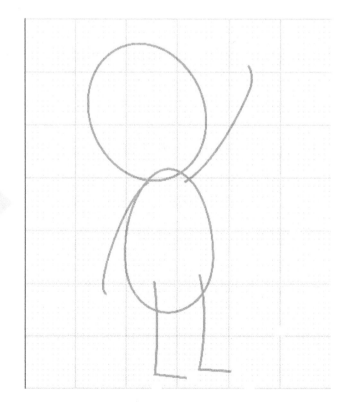

Come on!

Step 3

Step 4

Your turn!

She is sitting down.

Step 1

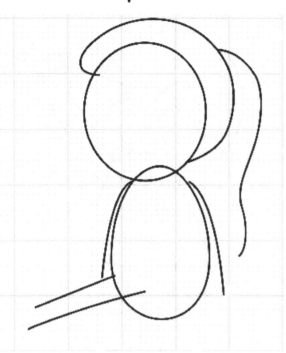

Step 2

Practice
with help

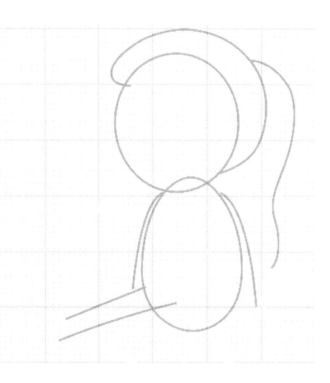

How are you?

Step 3

Step 4

Your turn!

He is thinking.

Step 1

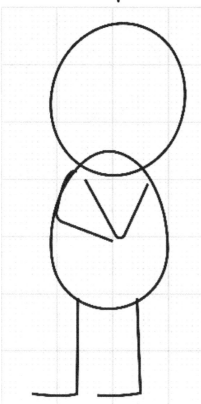

Step 2

Practice
with help

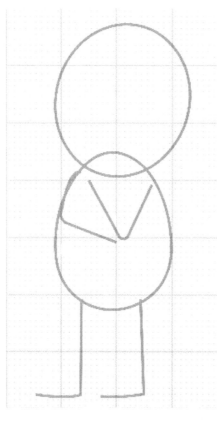

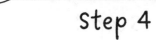

Where is she?

Step 3

Step 4

Your turn!

She's reading a book.

Step 1

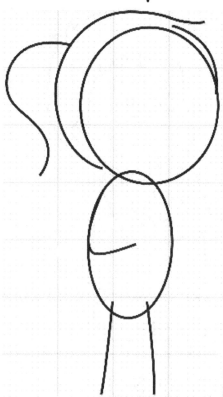

Step 2

Practice with help

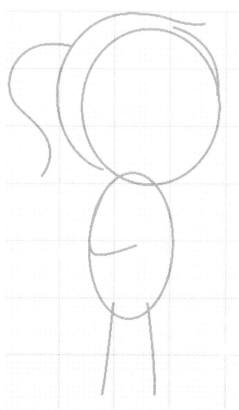

Interesting!

Step 3

Step 4

Your turn!

23

He's playing with a phone.

Step 1

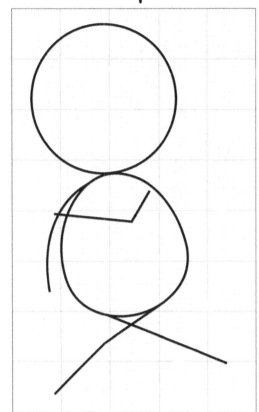

Step 2

Practice
with help

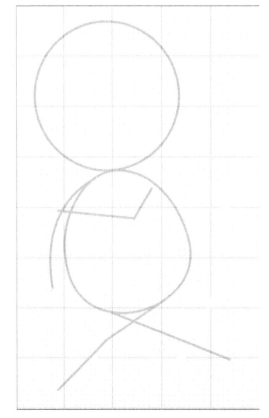

This is funny!

Step 3

Step 4

Your turn!

25

She is speaking.

Step 1

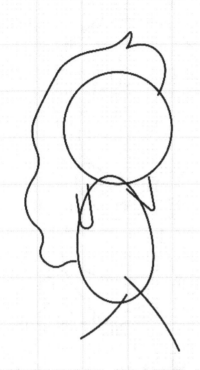

Step 2

Practice with help

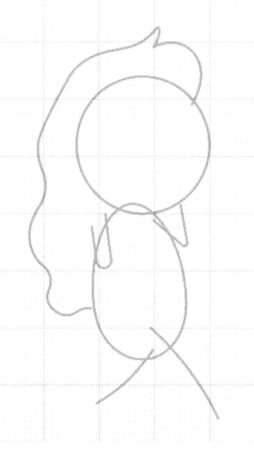

Hello!

Step 3

Step 4

Your turn!

He is pointing.

Step 1

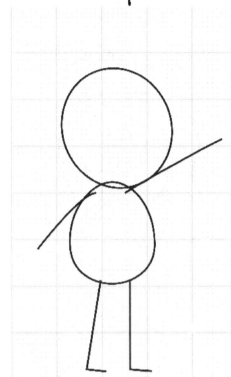

Step 2

Practice
with help

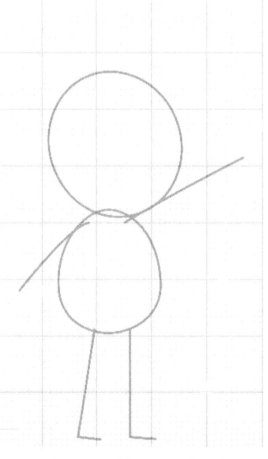

What's up?

Step 3

Step 4

Your turn!

She's drinking juice.

Step 1

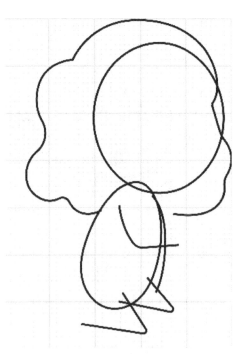

Step 2

Practice with help

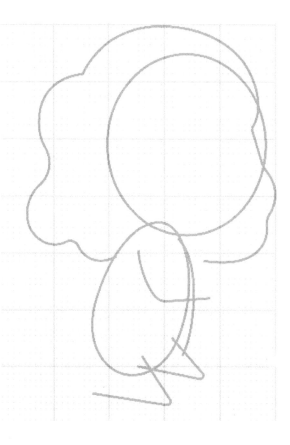

I like it!

Step 3

Step 4

Your turn!

He's kicking a ball.

Step 1

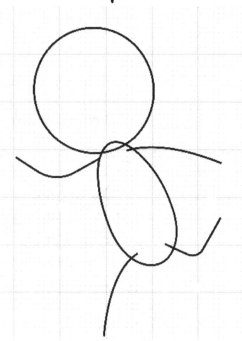

Step 2

Practice
with help

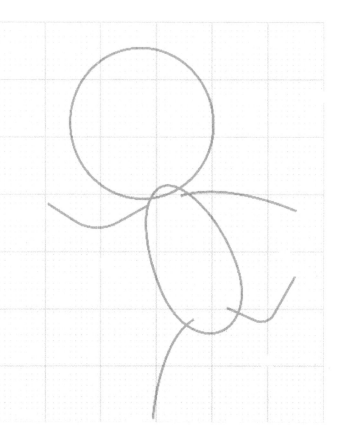

32

Let's play!

Step 3

Step 4

Your turn!

She's playing with a ball.

Step 1

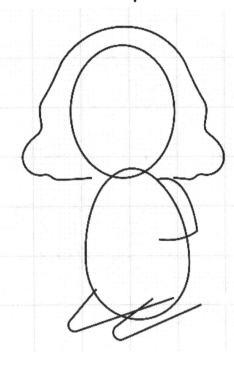

Step 2

Practice
with help

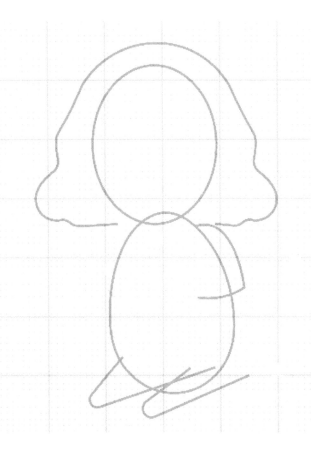

Step 3

Step 4

Your turn!

35

He's raising his hand.

Step 1

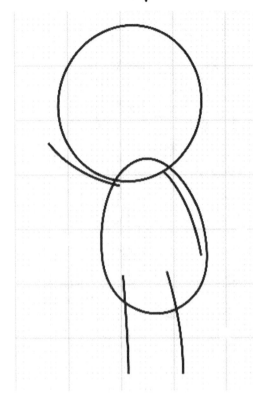

Step 2

Practice
with help

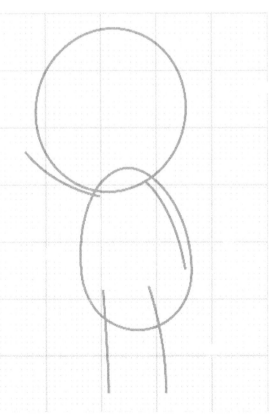

Hey!

Step 3

Step 4

Your turn!

She's receiving a gift.

Step 1

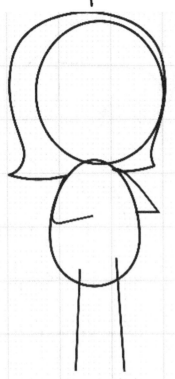

Step 2

Practice
with help

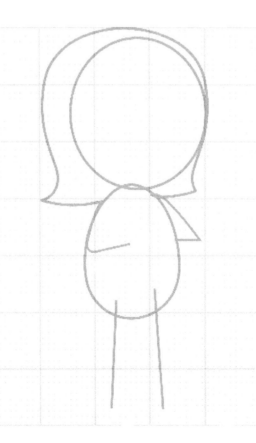

What a surprise!

Step 3

Step 4

Your turn!

He is waiting.

Step 1

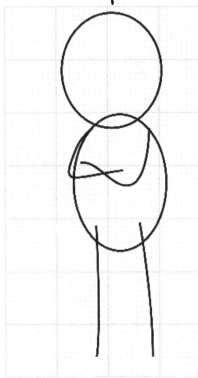

Step 2

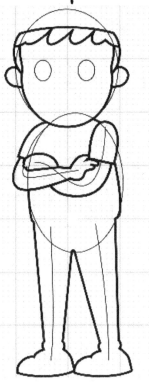

Practice
with help

Hey there!

Step 3

Step 4

Your turn!

She is yawning.

Step 1

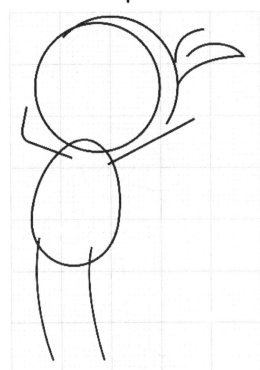

Step 2

Practice
with help

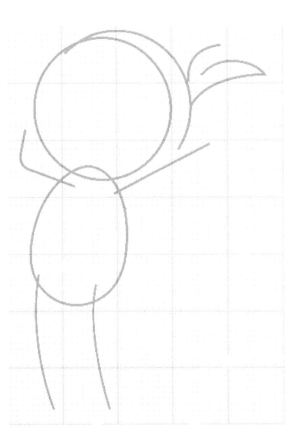

42

I'm sleepy!

Step 3

Step 4

Your turn!

He's flying a kite.

Step 1

Step 2

Practice
with help

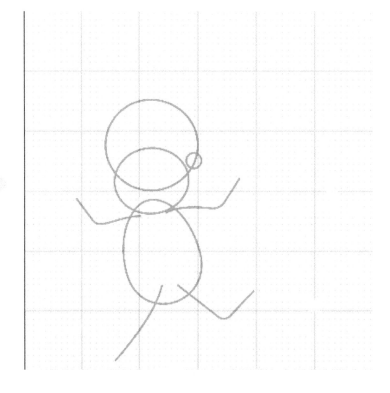

Step 3

Step 4

Your turn!

She is walking.

Step 1

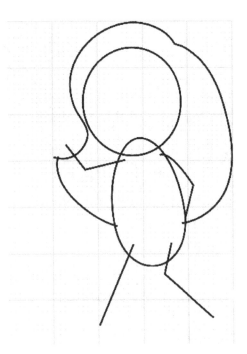

Step 2

Practice
with help

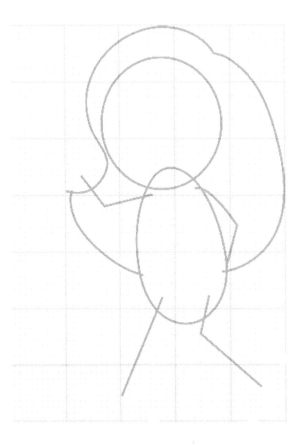

Good morning!

Step 3

Step 4

Your turn!

He's watching a bug.

Step 1

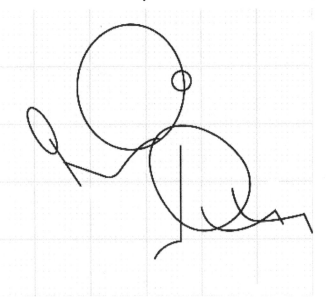

Step 2

Practice
with help

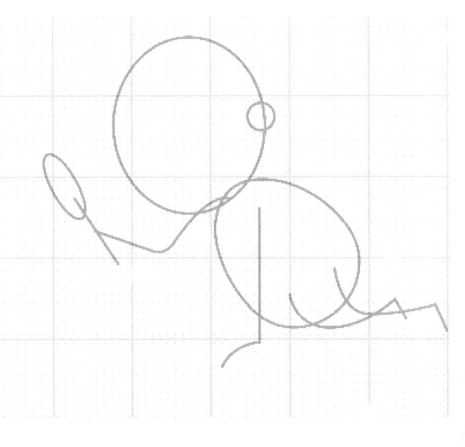

Step 3

Step 4

Your turn!

She's playing tennis.

Step 1

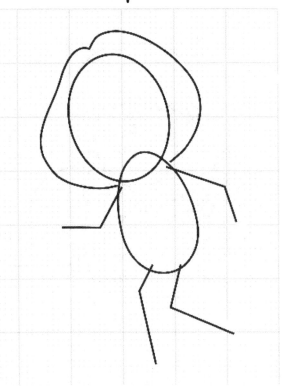

Step 2

Practice
with help

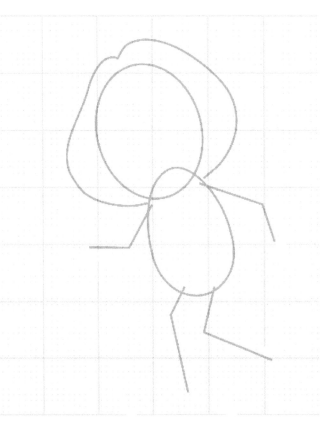

Good!

Step 3

Step 4

Your turn!

51

He is hula hooping.

Step 1

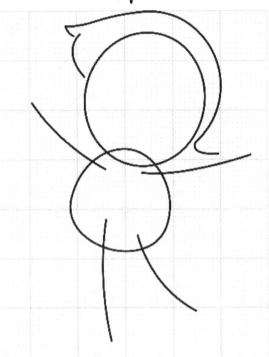

Step 2

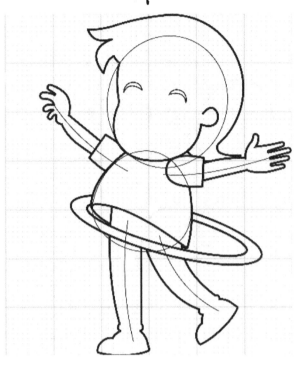

Practice
with help

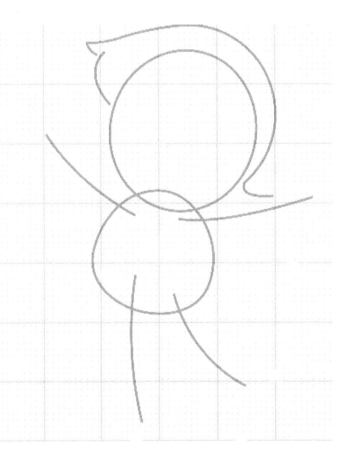

Amazing!

Step 3

Step 4

Your turn!

She is singing.

Step 1

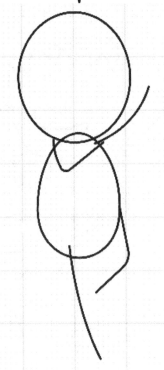

Step 2

Practice
with help

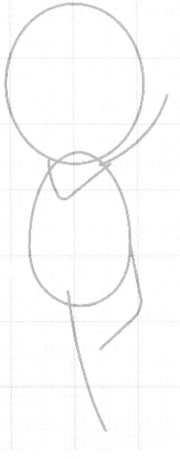

Hey there!

Step 3

Step 4

Your turn!

He is eating a burger.

Step 1

Step 2

Practice
with help

I'm hungry!

Step 3

Step 4

Your turn!

She is thinking.

Step 1

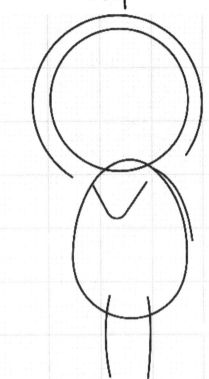

Step 2

Practice
with help

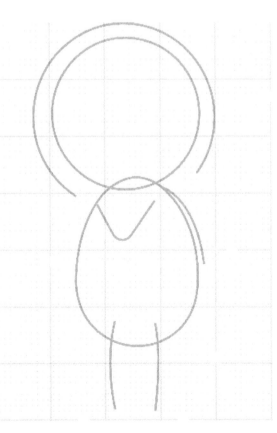

58

What's up?

Step 3

Step 4

Your turn!

He is stretching.

Step 1

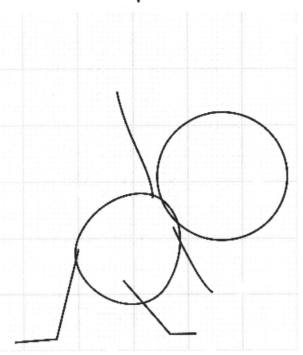

Step 2

Practice
with help

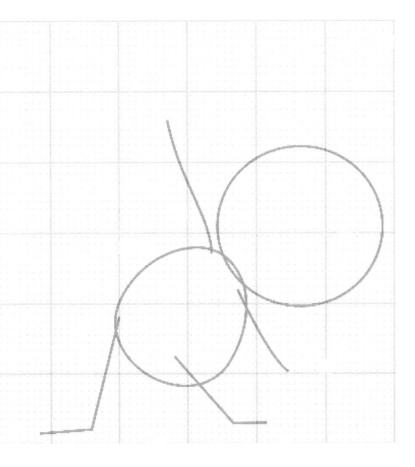

How's it going?

Step 3

Step 4

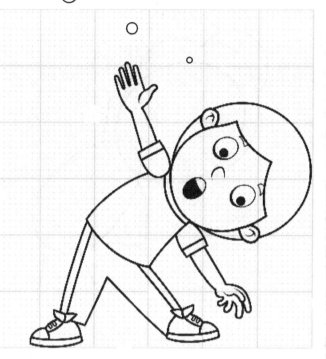

Your turn!

She is stretching.

Step 1

Step 2

Practice
with help

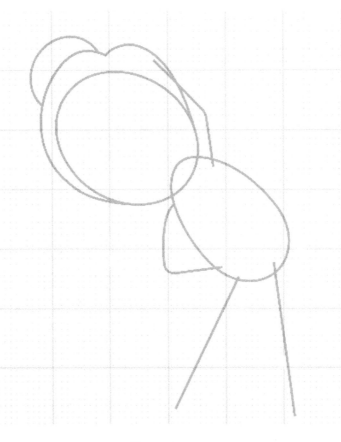

This is funny!

Step 3

Step 4

Your turn!

63

He is running.

Step 1

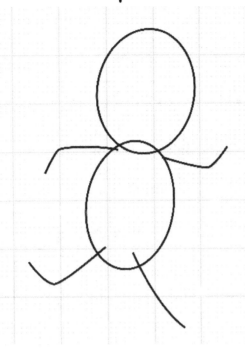

Step 2

Practice
with help

Good day!

Step 3

Step 4

Your turn!

She's playing with cubes.

Step 1

Step 2

Practice
with help

Step 3

Step 4

Your turn!

He is sitting down.

Step 1

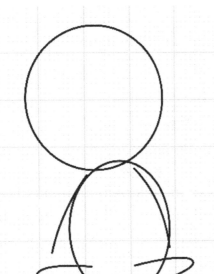

Step 2

Practice
with help

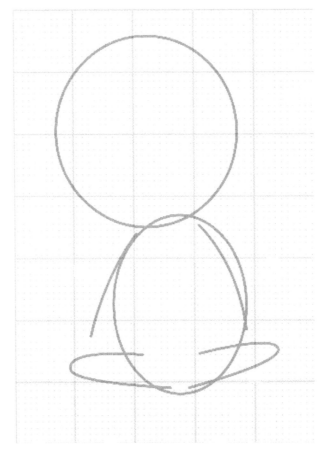

Step 3

Step 4

Hey there!

Your turn!

She's eating ice cream.

Step 1

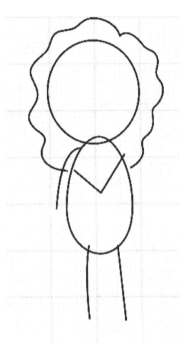

Step 2

Practice
with help

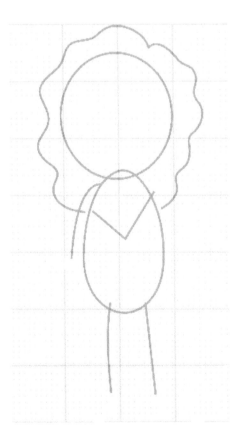

Delicious!

Step 3

Step 4

Your turn!

He's playing with a train.

Step 1

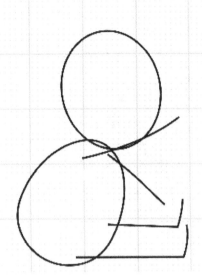

Step 2

Practice
with help

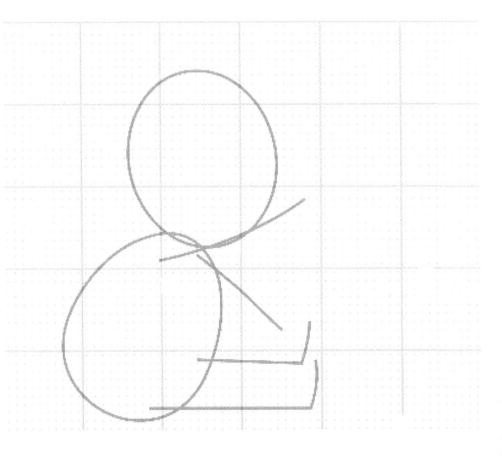

72

Good morning!

Step 3

Step 4

Your turn!

She is dancing.

Step 1

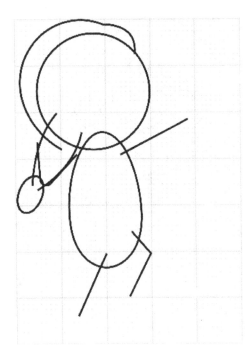

Step 2

Practice with help

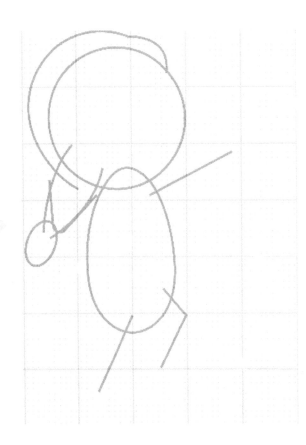

Step 3

Step 4

Your turn!

He is eating ice cream.

Step 1

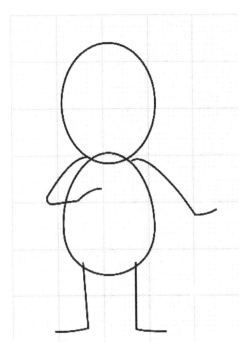

Step 2

Practice
with help

Yummy!

Step 3

Step 4

Your turn!

She's hugging her bear.

Step 1

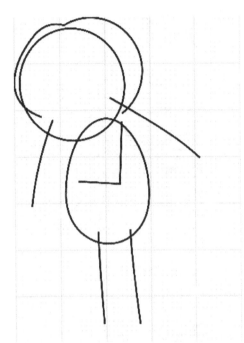

Step 2

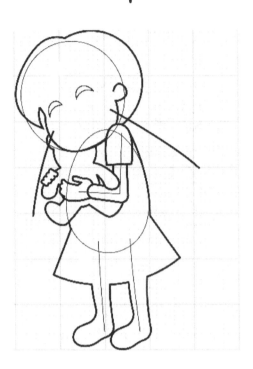

Practice
with help

Step 3

Step 4

Your turn!

79

Your support is important!

Dear customer,

We hope you enjoyed drawing People with this book. We would be very grateful if you leave us a positive review on Amazon.com. Thank you!

Sincerely,

Martha Blonde

Made in the USA
Las Vegas, NV
13 October 2024

96823236R00046